Shopping Addiction: How to Co... Spe...

AUTHOR:

Noah Felix Bennett

PUBLISHED BY:

Noah Felix Bennett

Copyright © 2025 - NostalgiaFindsBoutique™. All Rights Reserved.

This book and all related content are protected by copyright law. No part of this publication may be reproduced, distributed, stored in a retrieval system, or transmitted in any form or by any means—electronic, mechanical, photocopying, recording, or otherwise—without prior written permission from the author and publisher, except in the case of brief quotations used in reviews or articles with proper attribution.

Unauthorized reproduction, distribution, or commercial use of this work is strictly prohibited and may result in legal action. This book is licensed for individual use only, and resale or sharing without permission is not allowed.

All content, including text, graphics, formatting, and intellectual property, is the exclusive property of NostalgiaFindsBoutique™. Any unauthorized use, adaptation, or modification of this material is a violation of copyright laws and will be pursued to the fullest extent of the law.

For permissions, inquiries, or licensing requests, please contact: nostalgiafindsboutique@gmail.com

Disclaimer: The information provided in this book is for educational and informational purposes only. The author and publisher are not responsible for any actions taken based on the content of this book. Readers should use their own judgment and consult professionals when necessary. The author disclaims any liability for direct or indirect consequences resulting from the use or misuse of the information contained herein.

Shopping Addiction: How to Control Your Spending

Introduction: 4

Chapter 1: Recognizing the Problem – Are You a Shopaholic? 6

Chapter 2: Understanding the Triggers – Why Do You Overspend? 14

Chapter 3: Setting Clear Financial Goals – Creating a Strong "Why" 22

Chapter 4: Budgeting and Tracking Your Spending – Taking Back Control 29

Chapter 5: Changing Shopping Habits – Rewiring Your Brain 36

Chapter 6: Overcoming Emotional Dependence on Shopping 43

Chapter 7: Eliminating Debt and Staying Debt-Free 49

Chapter 8: Building a Sustainable and Balanced Lifestyle . 56

Conclusion 63

Introduction:

Welcome to Shopping Addiction: How to Control Your Spending. If you're reading this, it's because you've realized that shopping has become more than just a hobby—it's a habit that's affecting your financial stability and emotional well-being. You're not alone, and it's possible to break free from the grip of compulsive shopping.

This book will guide you from Point A (high addiction) to Point B (freedom from compulsive shopping), providing practical tools and strategies to help you regain control over your finances and emotional health. You will learn to:

- Recognize the signs of shopping addiction.
- Understand the triggers behind compulsive buying.
- Set financial goals and track your spending.
- Develop healthier shopping habits and emotional coping mechanisms.
- Eliminate debt and build a balanced, sustainable lifestyle.

Who This Book Is For

This book is for anyone who feels overwhelmed by shopping habits that have spiraled out of control—whether you're in debt, struggling with impulse buys, or simply seeking to regain financial independence.

A Word of Encouragement

Overcoming shopping addiction takes time and patience. But by committing to change, you can build a life where shopping no longer controls you. Every small step is progress, and you have the tools to make it happen.

Shopping Addiction: How to Control Your Spending

Let's begin this transformative journey toward a more balanced and fulfilling life. You've got this!

Chapter 1: Recognizing the Problem – Are You a Shopaholic?

The Psychology of Shopping Addiction

Shopping addiction, also known as compulsive buying disorder (CBD), is a behavioral addiction characterized by an overwhelming urge to shop and spend money, even when it leads to negative consequences. This compulsive behavior is driven by psychological, emotional, and sometimes even biological factors.

The Science Behind Shopping Addiction

At its core, shopping addiction is linked to the brain's reward system. When a person makes a purchase, the brain releases dopamine, a neurotransmitter associated with pleasure and reward. This creates a temporary sense of happiness and satisfaction. However, much like substance addiction, the brain craves repeated stimulation, leading to compulsive shopping behavior.

Individuals with shopping addiction often experience a "high" when they purchase new items, followed by guilt, regret, or financial distress. This cycle of emotional highs and lows reinforces the compulsive behavior, making it difficult to break free.

Emotional and Psychological Drivers

Several psychological and emotional factors contribute to shopping addiction, including:

- Stress and Anxiety: Many people use shopping as an escape from stress, loneliness, or emotional distress.

- Low Self-Esteem: Some individuals shop to feel better about themselves, associating material possessions with self-worth.

- Social Pressure and FOMO (Fear of Missing Out): Social media and advertising create an illusion that material goods equate to happiness and success, pressuring individuals to keep up with trends.

- Impulse Control Issues: Some people struggle with impulse control, making it difficult to resist urges to shop, even when they know the consequences.

The Role of Marketing and Consumerism

Retailers and advertisers take advantage of human psychology to encourage compulsive spending. Strategies such as limited-time discounts, "buy now, pay later" schemes, and targeted online ads create an illusion of urgency and necessity, often leading to impulsive purchases.

Recognizing the psychological aspects of shopping addiction is the first step toward understanding and overcoming compulsive spending habits.

Signs and Symptoms of Shopping Addiction

Identifying shopping addiction requires an honest evaluation of one's behaviors and spending habits. Here are some common signs and symptoms of shopping addiction:

Emotional Symptoms

• Feeling an overwhelming urge to shop, even when unnecessary.

• Experiencing euphoria or relief while shopping, followed by guilt or anxiety.

• Using shopping as a way to escape negative emotions or life problems.

Behavioral Symptoms

• Making impulsive or unnecessary purchases regularly.

• Hiding shopping habits from friends or family members.

• Lying about how much money is spent on shopping.

• Continuing to shop despite financial struggles or mounting debt.

Financial Symptoms

• Accumulating credit card debt due to excessive shopping.

• Feeling unable to control spending even when facing financial hardship.

• Justifying unnecessary purchases with excuses like "I deserve this" or "It was on sale."

Social and Relationship Impact

• Shopping habits causing strain in relationships.

• Avoiding social activities in favor of shopping.

- Feeling embarrassed or guilty about purchases but unable to stop.

The Cycle of Compulsive Shopping

Shopping addiction follows a distinct cycle:

1. Trigger: Stress, boredom, or external influence (advertisement, sale, social media trends) leads to the urge to shop.

2. Impulse Purchase: A compulsive shopping spree occurs, bringing temporary happiness.

3. Guilt & Regret: After the shopping high fades, feelings of guilt and regret set in.

4. Financial Consequences: Credit card debt, unpaid bills, or financial stress accumulate.

5. Repeat Behavior: The emotional distress caused by guilt leads to another shopping spree, repeating the cycle.

Recognizing these patterns in yourself or someone you know is crucial to taking steps toward change.

The Difference Between Healthy and Compulsive Shopping

Shopping is a normal part of life, but when does it cross the line into addiction? Understanding the difference between healthy and compulsive shopping can help distinguish between normal spending habits and an unhealthy dependency.

Healthy Shopping Habits

- Planned Purchases: Buying items after careful consideration and budgeting.

- Emotional Control: Shopping does not dictate mood or emotions.

- Budget Awareness: Staying within financial limits and avoiding debt.

- Occasional Treats: Making occasional indulgences without guilt or negative consequences.

Compulsive Shopping Habits

- Impulsive Buying: Making unplanned purchases without consideration.

- Emotional Dependence: Using shopping as a coping mechanism for stress or sadness.

- Financial Struggles: Accumulating debt or financial problems due to excessive spending.

- Inability to Stop: Feeling a loss of control over spending habits.

Key Questions to Ask Yourself

- Do I buy things I don't need to feel better emotionally?

- Do I often regret purchases but still continue shopping excessively?

- Have I tried to stop shopping excessively but failed?

- Do I experience stress, anxiety, or guilt because of my spending habits?

If the answers indicate compulsive shopping behavior, it may be time to take steps toward regaining control over spending habits.

Self-Assessment Quiz: How Severe Is Your Shopping Addiction?

This self-assessment quiz is designed to help identify whether you have compulsive shopping tendencies. Answer honestly.

Shopping Behavior Questions

1. How often do you shop for non-essential items?
- (A) Rarely
- (B) Occasionally
- (C) Frequently
- (D) Almost every day

2. Do you buy things to improve your mood or distract yourself from problems?
- (A) Never
- (B) Sometimes
- (C) Often
- (D) Always

3. Do you feel guilty or anxious after shopping?
- (A) Never
- (B) Occasionally
- (C) Frequently
- (D) Always

Financial and Emotional Impact Questions

4. Do you hide your shopping habits from family or friends?

- (A) Never
- (B) Sometimes
- (C) Often
- (D) Always

5. Have you ever been in debt because of shopping?

- (A) No
- (B) A small amount
- (C) Moderate debt
- (D) Significant debt

6. Do you feel out of control when shopping?

- (A) Never
- (B) Occasionally
- (C) Frequently
- (D) Always

Scoring

- 6-10 Points: No shopping addiction.
- 11-15 Points: Mild shopping addiction – may need to monitor habits.
- 16-20 Points: Moderate shopping addiction – consider making lifestyle changes.
- 21+ Points: Severe shopping addiction – seek professional guidance.

Taking this quiz can help determine if shopping addiction is a serious concern and whether steps need to be taken to regain control.

Conclusion

Recognizing shopping addiction is the first step toward overcoming it. Understanding its psychological roots, identifying symptoms, distinguishing healthy from compulsive shopping, and assessing personal behaviors are crucial in making a positive change. The next step is to work toward regaining financial and emotional control, which will be explored in the following chapters.

Chapter 2: Understanding the Triggers – Why Do You Overspend?

Emotional Triggers: Shopping as a Coping Mechanism

Many individuals struggling with shopping addiction turn to spending as a way to manage their emotions. Whether it is stress, anxiety, loneliness, or sadness, shopping can provide a temporary escape from negative feelings. However, using shopping as a coping mechanism can lead to financial distress, guilt, and even deeper emotional struggles.

The Emotional Connection to Shopping

Shopping triggers the brain's reward system, providing a short-term sense of pleasure. For those who struggle with emotional regulation, this instant gratification can feel like relief from emotional turmoil. Some common emotional reasons for compulsive shopping include:

•   Stress Relief: Shopping serves as a distraction from overwhelming stress, whether from work, relationships, or personal challenges.

•   Boredom: Many individuals shop simply to fill time or create excitement in their lives.

•   Loneliness and Depression: Buying new things can provide a fleeting sense of connection, self-worth, or validation.

- Low Self-Esteem: Some people shop to feel better about themselves, using material possessions as a measure of success or attractiveness.

The Cycle of Emotional Shopping

Emotional shopping follows a predictable cycle:

1. Emotional Discomfort: Feeling stressed, sad, bored, or lonely.

2. Impulse to Shop: Seeking immediate relief or distraction.

3. Temporary Satisfaction: Feeling better momentarily after making a purchase.

4. Guilt and Regret: Realizing the financial and emotional consequences of unnecessary spending.

5. Repeat Behavior: Facing new emotional challenges and resorting to shopping again.

Breaking Free from Emotional Shopping

To overcome emotional shopping, it is essential to develop healthier coping mechanisms. Some effective strategies include:

- Practicing Mindfulness: Becoming aware of emotions before making a purchase.

- Finding Alternative Activities: Engaging in hobbies, exercise, or social interactions instead of shopping.

- Journaling: Writing down emotions and triggers to identify patterns.

•   Seeking Support: Talking to a friend, therapist, or support group about emotional struggles instead of shopping.

Environmental Triggers: Sales, Advertisements, and Social Pressure

The environment plays a significant role in fueling shopping addiction. From aggressive marketing tactics to societal pressures, external influences often encourage excessive spending.

The Impact of Sales and Discounts

Retailers use psychological tactics to create a sense of urgency, making consumers believe they need to buy immediately. Common strategies include:

•   Limited-Time Offers: Flash sales, countdown timers, and one-day-only deals pressure shoppers into quick decisions.

•   Buy-One-Get-One-Free (BOGO): This strategy makes people feel like they are getting a better deal, leading to unnecessary purchases.

•   Discounted Items: Seeing a product on sale often convinces people they are "saving" money, even when they weren't planning to buy it in the first place.

The Influence of Advertisements and Social Media

Advertising is designed to trigger emotional responses and create desires that didn't previously exist. Influencers, celebrity endorsements, and targeted social media ads manipulate consumers into believing they need certain products to be happy, successful, or trendy.

Key ways advertisements influence shopping behavior:

• Emotional Manipulation: Ads associate products with happiness, luxury, or success.

• Fear of Missing Out (FOMO): Seeing others enjoying certain brands creates pressure to follow trends.

• Personalized Marketing: Online algorithms track user behavior and suggest products tailored to shopping habits, making purchases more tempting.

The Role of Social Pressure

Societal expectations and peer influence can also contribute to compulsive shopping. Whether it's keeping up with friends, following fashion trends, or impressing colleagues, many people feel pressure to spend beyond their means.

Strategies to Combat Environmental Triggers

• Unsubscribe from Marketing Emails: Reducing exposure to sales promotions can help limit impulse purchases.

• Limit Social Media Consumption: Reducing time spent on platforms that encourage consumerism can prevent unnecessary spending.

• Set a 48-Hour Rule: Before making a non-essential purchase, wait 48 hours to see if the desire remains.

• Shop with a List: Sticking to a planned shopping list can help avoid impulse buying.

Psychological Triggers: The Dopamine Effect of Buying

Shopping addiction is deeply connected to brain chemistry. The act of shopping releases dopamine, a neurotransmitter responsible for feelings of pleasure and reward. Understanding the science behind this process can help individuals take control of their shopping habits.

The Role of Dopamine in Shopping Addiction

When a person shops, their brain experiences a rush of dopamine, creating a temporary sense of excitement and satisfaction. This is similar to the way the brain reacts to drugs, alcohol, or gambling, which explains why some individuals become addicted to shopping.

The Cycle of Dopamine-Driven Shopping

1. Anticipation: Seeing a product online, in a store, or in an advertisement triggers excitement.

2. Purchase Decision: The act of buying releases a surge of dopamine, reinforcing the behavior.

3. Temporary Satisfaction: A brief period of happiness follows the purchase.

4. Dopamine Crash: The high fades, leading to feelings of emptiness or guilt.

5. Repeat Behavior: Seeking the next shopping "high" to regain the lost excitement.

Why Shopping Becomes Addictive

- Instant Gratification: Shopping provides an immediate reward, making it difficult to resist.

- Escapism: The dopamine rush allows people to temporarily escape from problems or stress.

- Reinforcement: The brain starts associating shopping with pleasure, making it harder to break the habit.

Strategies to Reduce Dopamine-Driven Shopping

- Delay Gratification: Waiting before making a purchase allows dopamine levels to settle, reducing impulsive decisions.

- Find Alternative Dopamine Boosters: Engaging in exercise, creative hobbies, or social interactions can provide similar pleasure without financial consequences.

- Use Cash Instead of Credit Cards: Physically handing over money makes spending feel more real, reducing impulse buys.

- Set Shopping Boundaries: Establishing rules like "no shopping unless necessary" can help rewire the brain's reward system.

Identifying Your Personal Triggers

Understanding personal triggers is the key to overcoming shopping addiction. While emotional, environmental, and psychological triggers affect many people, individual experiences and habits play a significant role in compulsive spending.

How to Identify Your Triggers

1. Keep a Shopping Journal: Record when, where, and why you make purchases. Look for patterns in emotional states, surroundings, or specific triggers.

2. Analyze Past Purchases: Reflect on unnecessary purchases and what motivated them.

3. Pay Attention to Shopping Urges: Notice what situations, emotions, or thoughts make you want to shop.

4. Ask Yourself Key Questions:

- Was I feeling stressed, bored, or lonely before shopping?
- Did an ad, email, or social media post make me want to buy?
- Am I shopping to fill an emotional void or because I genuinely need something?

Creating a Personal Action Plan

Once you have identified your triggers, you can take proactive steps to avoid them.

- Avoid Triggering Situations: If you tend to overspend at malls or online stores, limit exposure to these environments.
- Replace Shopping with Healthy Alternatives: Find activities that fulfill emotional needs without financial consequences.
- Establish Financial Goals: Having clear financial priorities can help resist impulsive spending.
- Seek Professional Help if Necessary: Therapy or financial counseling can provide guidance in managing shopping addiction.

Conclusion

By understanding the emotional, environmental, and psychological triggers behind compulsive shopping, individuals can take control of their spending habits. Identifying personal triggers and implementing practical strategies can lead to long-term financial and emotional well-being.

Chapter 3: Setting Clear Financial Goals – Creating a Strong "Why"

The Importance of Financial Awareness

Understanding your financial situation is the first step toward overcoming shopping addiction. Many individuals struggling with compulsive shopping avoid looking at their bank accounts or credit card statements because they feel overwhelmed or ashamed. However, financial awareness is crucial for making informed decisions and regaining control over spending habits.

Assessing Your Current Financial Situation

To develop financial awareness, you must start by evaluating your current financial standing. Here's how:

- Track Your Expenses: Write down every purchase you make for at least one month. Identify patterns and unnecessary spending.

- Review Your Debts: Calculate how much you owe on credit cards, loans, and other financial obligations.

- Analyze Your Income vs. Expenses: Compare your monthly income with your expenses to see if you are living within your means.

- Understand Your Net Worth: Subtract your liabilities from your assets to get a clear picture of your overall financial health.

The Psychological Impact of Financial Avoidance

Many shopaholics struggle with financial avoidance, where they refuse to confront their financial problems. This leads to:

- Increased anxiety and stress.
- A worsening cycle of debt.
- Feelings of hopelessness and low self-esteem.

Strategies to Develop Financial Awareness

1. Set a Weekly Finance Check-in: Dedicate 30 minutes each week to review your budget and expenses.

2. Use Budgeting Apps: Tools like Mint, YNAB, or PocketGuard can help track spending automatically.

3. Seek Financial Counseling: If debt has become unmanageable, speaking with a financial advisor can provide guidance.

4. Celebrate Small Wins: Every positive step you take, such as paying off a credit card or saving a set amount, should be acknowledged as progress.

Setting Short-Term and Long-Term Financial Goals

Once you have financial awareness, the next step is to set clear financial goals. These goals will serve as motivation to curb compulsive shopping and create a more stable future.

Why Setting Financial Goals Matters

Financial goals give you a purpose beyond shopping and help you:

- Stay motivated to control your spending.
- Build a sense of accomplishment when reaching milestones.
- Create a more secure financial future.

Short-Term Financial Goals

Short-term financial goals typically take a few months to a year to achieve. Examples include:

- Creating an Emergency Fund: Save at least three months' worth of expenses to avoid financial panic.
- Paying Off a Credit Card: Focus on clearing one debt at a time.
- Setting a Monthly Spending Limit: Establish a fixed budget for non-essential purchases.
- Starting a Savings Challenge: For example, saving $5 a day can add up significantly over time.

Long-Term Financial Goals

Long-term financial goals require more discipline but provide life-changing rewards. Examples include:

- Becoming Debt-Free: A plan to eliminate all outstanding debts within five years.
- Building an Investment Portfolio: Investing in stocks, bonds, or real estate for financial growth.

- Saving for Retirement: Contributing regularly to a retirement fund.

- Buying a Home or Car in Cash: Avoiding loans by saving ahead for major purchases.

Creating an Action Plan

1. Define Your Goals: Write down both short-term and long-term financial goals.

2. Set a Timeline: Assign a realistic deadline for each goal.

3. Break It into Steps: Outline small, manageable actions that will help you reach each goal.

4. Monitor Your Progress: Regularly review your achievements and adjust your strategies as needed.

Visualizing a Life Without Shopping Addiction

A powerful tool for overcoming shopping addiction is to visualize a life free from compulsive spending. Visualization helps reinforce the benefits of financial discipline and provides motivation to stay on track.

The Power of Visualization

Visualization is a mental technique where you create vivid images of your desired future. Studies have shown that people who visualize their goals are more likely to achieve them because the brain processes imagined experiences similarly to real ones.

How Shopping Addiction Limits Your Potential

Shopping addiction can prevent you from reaching your full potential by:

- Keeping you in constant debt.
- Preventing you from achieving meaningful life goals.
- Causing stress and anxiety over financial instability.
- Distracting you from more fulfilling activities and relationships.

Steps to Visualize Your Ideal Life

1. Picture Your Future Self: Imagine yourself living a debt-free, financially stable life.

2. Create a Vision Board: Collect images that represent your goals, such as a home, travel destinations, or a savings milestone.

3. Write a Future Narrative: Describe a day in your life five years from now, focusing on the benefits of financial freedom.

4. Practice Daily Visualization: Spend five minutes each morning imagining your ideal financial future.

Replacing Shopping with Meaningful Activities

Instead of shopping, invest time in activities that bring genuine joy and fulfillment, such as:

- Learning a new skill or hobby.
- Strengthening relationships with loved ones.
- Volunteering or giving back to the community.

- Traveling or experiencing new cultures.

Creating a Motivation Journal

A motivation journal is an effective way to track progress, reinforce positive habits, and stay committed to financial goals. It serves as a personal space to reflect on struggles and achievements, keeping you accountable on your journey.

Benefits of Keeping a Motivation Journal

- Tracks Spending Habits: Helps identify triggers and patterns.

- Provides Emotional Clarity: Writing about shopping urges can help you process emotions instead of spending impulsively.

- Encourages Mindful Spending: Keeping a log of every purchase can make you more conscious of unnecessary spending.

- Boosts Motivation: Reading past entries about progress can inspire continued commitment to financial goals.

What to Include in Your Motivation Journal

1. Daily Reflections: Write about your thoughts and emotions regarding money and shopping.

2. Success Stories: Record moments when you resisted impulse shopping and how it made you feel.

3. Financial Goals Checklist: Regularly update your goals and note progress.

4. Inspirational Quotes: Add quotes or affirmations that reinforce financial discipline.

5. Shopping Triggers Log: Identify and analyze what situations lead to shopping urges.

6. Savings Milestones: Celebrate achievements, such as reaching a savings target or paying off debt.

How to Use Your Motivation Journal Effectively

- Write in it daily or weekly.
- Review past entries to see progress.
- Use it as a tool for self-reflection before making a purchase.
- Set intentions for financial growth and remind yourself why you started this journey.

Conclusion

Setting clear financial goals is essential for overcoming shopping addiction. By developing financial awareness, establishing short-term and long-term goals, visualizing a life without shopping addiction, and maintaining a motivation journal, you can regain control over your finances and build a more fulfilling future. The key is to create a strong "why" that keeps you committed to financial stability and personal growth.

Chapter 4: Budgeting and Tracking Your Spending – Taking Back Control

The Power of a Zero-Based Budget

Budgeting is a fundamental tool for overcoming shopping addiction and regaining financial control. One of the most effective budgeting methods is the zero-based budget, where every dollar of your income is assigned to a specific purpose, ensuring that your spending aligns with your financial goals.

Understanding the Zero-Based Budget

A zero-based budget operates on a simple principle: Income - Expenses = Zero. This does not mean you spend every dollar you earn; instead, it means that each dollar has a designated role, whether for essentials, savings, or debt repayment.

Steps to Implement a Zero-Based Budget

1. Calculate Your Total Income: Include your salary, side gigs, or any other sources of income.

2. List All Monthly Expenses: Categorize them into essentials (rent, utilities, groceries) and non-essentials (subscriptions, dining out, entertainment).

3. Assign Every Dollar a Purpose: Allocate funds for necessities first, then for savings, debt reduction, and discretionary spending.

4. Adjust as Needed: If your expenses exceed your income, look for areas to cut back.

5.   Track Your Progress: Regularly review your budget and make adjustments.

Benefits of Zero-Based Budgeting

•   Increases Financial Awareness: Forces you to examine where every dollar goes.

•   Prevents Overspending: Limits unnecessary shopping by allocating funds in advance.

•   Encourages Savings and Debt Repayment: Prioritizes financial stability over impulsive spending.

•   Creates a Sense of Control: Eliminates guesswork in financial decisions.

By using a zero-based budget, you take an active role in managing your money, reducing the risk of shopping-related financial strain.

How to Track Your Expenses Effectively

Budgeting is ineffective if you do not track your spending habits. Expense tracking helps identify problem areas, enabling better financial decision-making.

The Importance of Expense Tracking

Tracking your expenses provides insights into:

•   Spending Patterns: Identifies categories where you overspend.

•   Hidden Costs: Uncovers small expenses that add up over time.

•   Budget Adjustments: Helps refine your budget based on actual spending.

Methods for Tracking Expenses

1. Manual Expense Logs: Use a notebook or spreadsheet to record every purchase.

2. Mobile Apps: Budgeting apps like Mint, YNAB, or PocketGuard automate tracking.

3. Bank Statements: Regularly review statements to categorize transactions.

4. Receipt Collection: Keep receipts and review them weekly.

5. Daily Expense Review: Set aside 5–10 minutes each day to log your spending.

How to Stay Consistent

- Make It a Habit: Integrate tracking into your daily routine.

- Use Alerts and Reminders: Set notifications for budget limits.

- Analyze Trends: Review expenses at the end of each month to adjust future budgets.

Tracking expenses effectively ensures that your financial goals remain on course, helping to curb impulsive shopping habits.

The 48-Hour Rule: Delaying Purchases to Reduce Impulse Buying

Impulse buying is one of the biggest challenges in overcoming shopping addiction. The 48-hour rule is a simple but powerful strategy to control unnecessary spending.

What Is the 48-Hour Rule?

The 48-hour rule involves waiting at least 48 hours before making a non-essential purchase. This delay allows you to:

- Evaluate Need vs. Want: Helps determine if the purchase is truly necessary.

- Avoid Emotional Spending: Reduces the impact of emotional triggers.

- Find Alternatives: Encourages you to explore options that don't involve spending.

- Stay on Budget: Prevents impulsive purchases from disrupting financial plans.

How to Implement the 48-Hour Rule

1. Identify a Shopping Urge: When you feel the desire to buy something, pause immediately.

2. Write It Down: List the item and its cost in a notebook or phone note.

3. Wait 48 Hours: Avoid purchasing during this period.

4. Reevaluate the Purchase: After 48 hours, ask yourself:

- Do I still want or need this item?

- Can I afford it without breaking my budget?

- Will this add long-term value to my life?

5. Make a Decision: If the item is still a priority and fits within your budget, buy it mindfully; otherwise, let it go.

Enhancing the Effectiveness of the 48-Hour Rule

•   Use Wish Lists: Instead of buying immediately, add items to a list and revisit them later.

•   Unsubscribe from Shopping Emails: Reduce exposure to sales and promotions.

•   Block Shopping Websites: Limit access to online stores during vulnerable moments.

•   Replace Shopping with Other Activities: Engage in hobbies, exercise, or social interactions instead.

Practicing the 48-hour rule transforms your relationship with spending, helping you develop mindful purchasing habits.

Using Cash-Only Methods and Envelope Budgeting

Digital transactions make spending easier and more detached from reality. Switching to cash-based spending methods can help reinforce financial discipline.

The Power of Using Cash

•   Creates a Physical Limit: Once cash is gone, spending stops.

•   Increases Awareness: Physically handling money makes spending more tangible.

•   Reduces Impulse Purchases: Limits spur-of-the-moment buying decisions.

The Envelope Budgeting System

Envelope budgeting involves dividing cash into labeled envelopes for different spending categories, preventing overspending in any one area.

How to Implement Envelope Budgeting

1. Determine Spending Categories: Common categories include groceries, entertainment, dining out, and transportation.

2. Set Budget Amounts: Allocate specific cash amounts to each envelope.

3. Use Only the Cash in Each Envelope: Once an envelope is empty, wait until the next budget cycle before spending again.

4. Adjust Monthly Allocations: Review your spending habits and refine amounts as needed.

Cash vs. Card Spending

Aspect	Cash-Only Method	Credit/Debit Cards
Spending Control	High – Limited by physical cash	Low – Easy to overspend
Awareness	Strong – Tangible money exchange	Weak – Digital transactions feel less real
Impulse Buying	Reduced – Forces mindful purchases	Increased – Instant transactions

Aspect	Cash-Only Method	Credit/Debit Cards
Budgeting	Simple – Envelopes show clear limits	Complex – Requires tracking expenses manually or via apps

Alternatives to Physical Cash

For those who prefer digital transactions, prepaid debit cards or separate bank accounts for each category can mimic the envelope budgeting system.

By using cash-only methods and envelope budgeting, you gain better control over your spending habits, making it easier to resist shopping temptations.

Conclusion

Budgeting and tracking spending are essential steps in overcoming shopping addiction. By adopting a zero-based budget, monitoring expenses, implementing the 48-hour rule, and using cash-based methods, you create a structured approach to financial discipline. Taking back control of your finances will not only reduce compulsive shopping but also pave the way for long-term financial freedom and peace of mind.

Chapter 5: Changing Shopping Habits – Rewiring Your Brain

Learning the Difference Between Needs and Wants

One of the fundamental steps in overcoming shopping addiction is developing a clear understanding of needs versus wants. Many shopaholics justify unnecessary purchases by blurring the line between these two concepts.

Defining Needs vs. Wants

•   Needs are essential for survival and well-being. These include housing, food, healthcare, and basic clothing.

•   Wants are non-essential items that enhance comfort or status, such as designer clothing, luxury items, or frequent dining out.

How to Differentiate Between the Two

1.   Pause Before Purchasing – Ask yourself: Is this item essential for my well-being, or do I just desire it?

2.   Assess Usage – Will this item provide long-term value, or is it an impulse buy?

3.   Consider Consequences – What happens if you don't buy it? If the answer is nothing significant, it's likely a want.

Strategies to Prioritize Needs Over Wants

•   Create a Needs-Only Budget for essentials.

- Delay gratification—wait 48 hours before purchasing non-essential items.

- Ask yourself: Can I borrow or repurpose something I already own instead?

- Use a visual spending tracker to differentiate between needs and wants.

Understanding the difference between needs and wants rewires your shopping mindset, helping you make more conscious and responsible purchasing decisions.

Creating a Shopping List and Sticking to It

A shopping list is a powerful tool for controlling spending and avoiding unnecessary purchases. It provides structure and discipline when shopping, helping you buy only what you truly need.

Why Shopping Lists Work

- Prevents Impulse Buying – If it's not on the list, you don't buy it.

- Saves Time and Money – You shop efficiently and avoid unnecessary expenses.

- Encourages Mindful Spending – Forces you to plan purchases in advance.

How to Create an Effective Shopping List

1. Assess Your Needs: Before heading out, review what you truly require.

2. Categorize Items: Divide the list into essentials (groceries, household items) and non-essentials (clothing, accessories).

3. Set a Spending Limit: Allocate a budget and ensure you don't exceed it.

4. Use a Written or Digital List: Utilize apps like Google Keep, Evernote, or a simple notepad.

Sticking to Your List

•   Shop with Purpose: Go in, get what you need, and leave.

•   Avoid Browsing: Stay away from unnecessary aisles or sections.

•   Use Cash Instead of Cards: Physically limiting money reinforces discipline.

•   Hold Yourself Accountable: Reward yourself for sticking to the list but not with shopping!

By following a strict shopping list, you reduce the likelihood of succumbing to shopping triggers and maintain control over your finances.

Avoiding Temptation: Unsubscribing from Marketing Emails and Ads

Retailers use aggressive marketing tactics to lure customers into unnecessary purchases. Removing these shopping triggers is a key step in rewiring your brain to avoid impulsive shopping.

Why Marketing Emails and Ads Are Dangerous

•   Create a False Sense of Urgency – "Limited time offer!" makes you feel like you'll miss out.

•	Trigger Emotional Spending – Discounts and promotions exploit emotions, making purchases feel justifiable.

•	Encourage Comparison and Envy – Social media ads create a desire to keep up with trends.

How to Remove Marketing Triggers

1.	Unsubscribe from Retail Emails: Use services like Unroll.Me to bulk unsubscribe.

2.	Turn Off Notifications: Disable app notifications from shopping platforms.

3.	Use Ad Blockers: Install browser extensions to block ads.

4.	Unfollow Influencers Promoting Excessive Shopping: Reduce exposure to lifestyle influencers who encourage buying.

5.	Limit Social Media Usage: Platforms like Instagram and TikTok bombard users with targeted ads.

Replacing Shopping with Healthier Activities

•	Practice Mindful Browsing – Instead of browsing sales, read financial literacy blogs.

•	Replace Shopping with Productive Hobbies – Engage in creative pursuits, exercise, or social activities.

•	Use Positive Reinforcement – Reward yourself for avoiding impulse buys with experiences, not purchases.

By eliminating exposure to advertisements and marketing strategies, you regain control over your spending impulses and reduce unnecessary temptations.

Finding Healthier Alternatives to Shopping

For many shopaholics, shopping isn't just about acquiring goods—it's an emotional escape. Finding healthier, non-shopping-related activities can replace the dopamine rush of buying new things.

Why Shopping Becomes a Habit

•   Stress Relief – Shopping provides temporary relief from anxiety or boredom.

•   Instant Gratification – The act of purchasing releases dopamine, reinforcing compulsive behavior.

•   Social Connection – Many people shop as a way to bond with friends or family.

Healthier Alternatives to Shopping

1. Exercise and Physical Activities

•   Join a gym, take yoga classes, or go for daily walks.

•   Exercise provides a natural dopamine boost, reducing the urge to shop.

2. Creative Outlets

•   Try painting, writing, photography, or crafting as a new hobby.

•   Creative activities stimulate the brain and provide a sense of fulfillment.

3. Volunteer Work

•   Helping others through charity work or community service brings deep satisfaction.

- Shifts focus from materialistic desires to meaningful contributions.

4. Mindfulness and Meditation

- Practicing mindfulness helps reduce impulsive behaviors and emotional spending.
- Meditation, journaling, and gratitude exercises can replace the thrill of shopping.

5. Social Engagement Without Spending

- Host game nights, attend free events, or enjoy outdoor activities with friends.
- Shopping should not be the default social activity.

How to Make These Alternatives Sustainable

- Schedule Activities in Advance: Plan your week with fulfilling hobbies.
- Join a Support Group: Connecting with others on the same journey enhances accountability.
- Track Your Progress: Keep a journal of money saved and emotions experienced.

Replacing shopping with healthier habits transforms your mindset, allowing you to find true fulfillment without relying on material possessions.

Conclusion

Changing shopping habits requires rewiring your brain to approach spending in a more conscious and disciplined way. By distinguishing needs from wants, using structured shopping lists, eliminating shopping triggers, and replacing compulsive buying with healthier activities, you gradually regain control over your financial and emotional well-being.

Breaking free from shopping addiction is not about deprivation—it's about gaining freedom from compulsive habits and embracing a more fulfilling, financially stable life.

Chapter 6: Overcoming Emotional Dependence on Shopping

Recognizing Emotional Spending Patterns

Shopping addiction is often fueled by emotional spending, where purchases are driven by feelings rather than necessity. Recognizing these patterns is the first step toward breaking free from compulsive shopping habits.

Common Emotional Triggers for Shopping

1.	Stress and Anxiety: Shopping provides a temporary escape from overwhelming emotions.

2.	Boredom and Loneliness: Many people shop to fill emotional voids.

3.	Low Self-Esteem: Buying new items can create a false sense of self-worth.

4.	Happiness and Excitement: Celebratory shopping can become a habit.

5.	Social Influence: Pressure from friends, influencers, and advertisements can push you to shop unnecessarily.

How to Identify Your Emotional Spending Triggers

•	Keep a Spending Journal: Track your purchases and note the emotions felt before, during, and after buying.

•	Pause Before Buying: Ask yourself: Am I shopping because I need this or because I'm feeling a certain way?

- Rate Your Purchases: On a scale of 1-10, assess if an item is essential or emotionally driven.

Breaking the Emotional Spending Cycle

- Acknowledge Your Feelings: Recognize when emotions are driving your desire to shop.

- Find Alternative Comforts: Replace shopping with healthier ways to cope.

- Set Financial Boundaries: Implement spending rules to prevent impulse buying.

Recognizing emotional spending is essential to overcoming shopping addiction and regaining control over your financial and emotional well-being.

Finding New Coping Mechanisms for Stress and Anxiety

If shopping has been your primary way of dealing with stress and anxiety, it's crucial to replace it with healthier coping mechanisms.

Healthy Alternatives to Shopping

1. Exercise: Physical activity releases endorphins, reducing stress naturally.

2. Meditation and Deep Breathing: Mindfulness techniques help you stay present and reduce emotional impulses.

3. Journaling: Writing down your thoughts and emotions can help process feelings instead of suppressing them with shopping.

4. Engaging in a Hobby: Channel your energy into painting, writing, cooking, or learning something new.

5. Spending Time in Nature: Walking, hiking, or simply sitting in a park can calm the mind.

How to Make These New Habits Stick

•   Schedule Activities: Plan workouts, meditation, or journaling time in your daily routine.

•   Replace Triggers with Positive Actions: Instead of visiting shopping sites, engage in an activity that relaxes you.

•   Reward Yourself Without Spending: Treat yourself with self-care, not shopping.

Replacing shopping with constructive coping mechanisms will help you manage emotions in a way that nurtures long-term well-being.

Practicing Mindfulness and Gratitude

Mindfulness and gratitude are powerful tools in overcoming emotional shopping. They help shift focus from material possessions to appreciating what you already have.

The Role of Mindfulness in Reducing Shopping Urges

•   Increases Awareness: Helps you recognize emotional triggers before acting on them.

•   Encourages Thoughtful Decisions: Reduces impulsive buying by promoting deliberate spending choices.

• Enhances Self-Control: Strengthens the ability to resist shopping temptations.

Mindfulness Techniques for Overcoming Shopping Addiction

1. Practice Deep Breathing: When tempted to shop, take a few deep breaths and assess your emotions.

2. Use the Five-Minute Rule: Before making a purchase, wait five minutes and ask yourself if you truly need the item.

3. Engage in Present Activities: Redirect your focus to an enjoyable, non-shopping-related activity.

4. Avoid Shopping on Autopilot: Be conscious of your purchases and the reasons behind them.

Cultivating Gratitude to Reduce Materialistic Desires

• Keep a Gratitude Journal: Write down three things you're grateful for daily.

• Appreciate What You Own: Take inventory of what you already have and recognize its value.

• Give Back: Volunteering shifts focus from material possessions to meaningful experiences.

By integrating mindfulness and gratitude into your life, you'll develop a more fulfilling and emotionally stable approach to spending.

Building a Support System (Family, Friends, or Support Groups)

Overcoming shopping addiction is easier with a strong support system. Surrounding yourself with people who understand and encourage your journey can make a significant difference.

The Importance of a Support System

• Accountability: Helps you stay on track and resist shopping urges.

• Emotional Support: Provides comfort during challenging moments.

• Shared Experiences: Learning from others who have overcome similar struggles can be inspiring.

Who Can Be Part of Your Support System?

1. Family and Friends: Share your goals with loved ones and ask for their encouragement.

2. Support Groups: Join groups like Debtors Anonymous or online forums for shopaholics.

3. Financial Coaches or Therapists: Seek professional guidance to develop healthier spending habits.

4. Accountability Partners: Find someone who can check in with you regularly about your progress.

How to Build and Maintain Your Support System

• Be Open About Your Struggles: Honest conversations lead to understanding and encouragement.

- Set Boundaries with Shopping Enthusiasts: Avoid spending too much time with people who encourage impulsive shopping.

- Celebrate Small Wins Together: Acknowledge progress with non-shopping rewards.

- Attend Regular Meetings or Check-Ins: Consistent support fosters long-term change.

A strong support system provides the motivation and reassurance needed to overcome shopping addiction for good.

Conclusion

Breaking free from emotional dependence on shopping requires awareness, healthier coping mechanisms, mindfulness, gratitude, and a strong support system. By recognizing emotional spending patterns, finding better ways to manage stress, practicing mindfulness, and surrounding yourself with supportive people, you'll develop a more intentional and fulfilling relationship with money and possessions.

Shopping addiction isn't about the items—it's about the emotions behind them. By addressing these emotions head-on, you'll reclaim control over your finances and emotional well-being, paving the way for a healthier, happier life.

Chapter 7: Eliminating Debt and Staying Debt-Free

Understanding the Consequences of Shopping-Related Debt

Excessive shopping often leads to significant financial burdens, affecting not only your bank account but also your overall well-being. Understanding the consequences of shopping-related debt can serve as a wake-up call and motivation to take control of your financial future.

Financial Consequences

1. Accumulating High-Interest Debt: Credit card balances grow rapidly due to compounding interest.

2. Difficulty Covering Basic Needs: Excessive debt can limit your ability to afford essentials like rent, utilities, and groceries.

3. Lower Credit Score: Missed payments and high credit utilization negatively impact your creditworthiness.

4. Limited Financial Freedom: Being in debt reduces opportunities for investment, savings, and life experiences.

Emotional and Psychological Consequences

1. Stress and Anxiety: Constant worry about debt creates mental and emotional distress.

2. Guilt and Regret: Overspending often leads to feelings of shame and frustration.

3. Strained Relationships: Financial strain can cause conflicts with family, friends, and partners.

4. Depression and Hopelessness: Persistent debt can make you feel trapped and overwhelmed.

Taking Accountability

- Acknowledge the Problem: Recognizing the impact of debt is the first step toward change.
- Assess Your Financial Situation: List all debts, interest rates, and monthly payments.
- Commit to Change: Develop a mindset focused on financial responsibility.

Understanding these consequences will help you stay motivated to eliminate debt and adopt healthier financial habits.

Creating a Debt Repayment Plan

Once you recognize the dangers of debt, the next step is to develop a structured repayment plan. Having a strategy in place will help you regain control over your finances and steadily work toward a debt-free life.

Steps to Creating a Debt Repayment Plan

1. List All Your Debts: Write down balances, interest rates, and minimum payments.
2. Choose a Repayment Strategy:
- Debt Snowball Method: Pay off the smallest debts first for quick wins.
- Debt Avalanche Method: Focus on debts with the highest interest rates to save money long-term.
3. Set a Realistic Budget: Allocate a fixed amount toward debt payments each month.

4. Cut Unnecessary Expenses: Reduce spending on non-essentials to free up money for debt payments.

5. Increase Income Streams: Consider side jobs, freelancing, or selling unused items.

6. Negotiate with Creditors: Some lenders offer lower interest rates or flexible payment plans if you ask.

7. Automate Payments: Set up automatic transfers to avoid missed payments and late fees.

Staying Motivated During Debt Repayment

- Track Progress: Use apps or a spreadsheet to monitor debt reduction.
- Celebrate Small Wins: Reward yourself when you hit major milestones (without shopping!).
- Remind Yourself of the Benefits: Visualize the financial freedom you'll gain once you're debt-free.

By following a structured repayment plan, you'll steadily eliminate debt and build a stronger financial future.

Learning How to Say "No" to Unnecessary Spending

Breaking free from shopping addiction requires learning to say "no" to unnecessary expenses and resisting societal pressure to buy more than you need.

Why It's Hard to Say No

- Social Expectations: Friends or family may encourage spending on outings or gifts.

- Marketing Tactics: Retailers create urgency with limited-time sales and discounts.
- Emotional Attachments: Shopping can feel like a reward or coping mechanism.

Strategies to Say No to Impulse Spending

1. Practice the 48-Hour Rule: Before making a purchase, wait two days to evaluate its necessity.
2. Use a Shopping Mantra: Repeat affirmations like "I control my money, my money doesn't control me."
3. Create Spending Rules: Only buy non-essential items after meeting savings goals.
4. Avoid Shopping Triggers: Stay away from malls, unsubscribe from store emails, and block ads.
5. Be Honest with Friends and Family: Let them know you're committed to financial health.
6. Carry Limited Cash: Use only the amount necessary for essential expenses.
7. Redirect Temptations: Instead of shopping, engage in a productive hobby or exercise.

Handling Social Pressure

- Suggest Free or Low-Cost Activities: Propose alternatives like home-cooked meals, outdoor activities, or game nights.
- Set Boundaries: Politely decline invitations that encourage unnecessary spending.
- Surround Yourself with Like-Minded People: Engage with those who support your financial goals.

By mastering the art of saying no, you'll break free from impulsive spending and develop a mindset focused on financial well-being.

Avoiding Credit Card Traps and High-Interest Loans

Credit cards and high-interest loans often play a major role in shopping-related debt. Learning how to avoid financial pitfalls will help you stay debt-free.

The Dangers of Credit Cards and Loans

• High-Interest Rates: Balances grow rapidly if not paid in full each month.

• Minimum Payments Trap: Paying only the minimum extends debt for years.

• Hidden Fees: Late payments, annual fees, and overdraft charges increase overall debt.

• False Sense of Security: Easy access to credit encourages overspending.

How to Use Credit Cards Responsibly

1. Pay the Full Balance Each Month: Avoid interest charges by clearing balances before the due date.

2. Use Credit Only for Essentials: Limit credit card usage to bills or necessary expenses.

3. Set a Credit Limit: Lower your spending limit to avoid excessive debt.

4. Track Credit Card Usage: Monitor statements to prevent unauthorized charges or overspending.

5. Avoid Store Credit Cards: These often have higher interest rates and encourage unnecessary purchases.

How to Stay Away from High-Interest Loans

•   Avoid Payday Loans: These come with extreme interest rates that trap borrowers in cycles of debt.

•   Consider Alternative Lending Options: Look for low-interest personal loans or credit union assistance.

•   Improve Credit Score: A higher score qualifies you for lower interest rates.

•   Build an Emergency Fund: Having savings prevents reliance on loans in times of crisis.

What to Do If You're Already in Credit Card Debt

1.   Stop Using Credit Cards: Shift to cash or debit to avoid accumulating more debt.

2.   Prioritize High-Interest Debt: Use the debt avalanche method to pay down expensive balances first.

3.   Look for Balance Transfer Options: Some banks offer low or zero-interest transfers for limited periods.

4.   Negotiate with Credit Card Companies: Ask for reduced interest rates or alternative repayment plans.

By avoiding credit traps and managing credit responsibly, you'll protect yourself from future financial stress and maintain long-term financial stability.

Conclusion

Eliminating debt and staying debt-free requires awareness, discipline, and strategic financial planning. By understanding the consequences of debt, creating a solid repayment plan, learning to say no to unnecessary spending, and avoiding credit card traps, you'll regain financial control and build a stable, debt-free future. Financial freedom isn't about deprivation—it's about empowerment and making choices that align with your long-term goals.

Chapter 8: Building a Sustainable and Balanced Lifestyle

Shifting Your Focus to Experiences Instead of Material Goods

Overcoming shopping addiction isn't just about restricting spending—it's about replacing shopping with meaningful experiences that bring long-term fulfillment. Many people shop out of habit, boredom, or emotional need, but shifting the focus from material goods to valuable experiences can lead to a more satisfying and balanced life.

Why Experiences Matter More Than Material Possessions

1. Long-Lasting Happiness: Studies show that experiences create lasting joy, whereas material purchases lose their appeal over time.

2. Stronger Social Connections: Activities with friends and family deepen relationships more than material gifts.

3. Personal Growth: Experiences such as travel, education, and volunteering lead to self-improvement and new perspectives.

4. Less Clutter, More Freedom: Focusing on experiences reduces the need for excessive possessions, making life simpler and more enjoyable.

Ways to Shift from Shopping to Experiences

- Travel and Exploration: Instead of buying new clothes, plan a weekend trip to a nearby town or explore nature.

- Cultural Activities: Attend live music performances, theater shows, or museums instead of shopping at malls.

- Educational Experiences: Invest in online courses, workshops, or books that enrich your knowledge.

- Quality Time with Loved Ones: Host game nights, cook together, or take part in outdoor activities.

Creating a Lifestyle Around Experiences

- Set an Experience Budget: Allocate funds for hobbies, travel, or educational pursuits instead of shopping.

- Track Emotional Benefits: Reflect on how experiences make you feel compared to impulse shopping.

- Surround Yourself with Like-Minded People: Spend time with individuals who value experiences over material goods.

By focusing on experiences, you'll cultivate a richer, more meaningful life without the need for unnecessary shopping.

Developing New Hobbies That Don't Involve Shopping

A major challenge in overcoming shopping addiction is filling the time and emotional void left behind. Developing new hobbies can replace the need to shop and bring joy, creativity, and fulfillment into your life.

Why Hobbies Help Break the Shopping Cycle

1. Distraction from Urges: Engaging in a hobby keeps your mind occupied, reducing impulsive shopping thoughts.

2. Boosting Self-Worth: Creative and productive hobbies provide a sense of accomplishment.

3. Reducing Stress and Anxiety: Activities such as exercise and art can be therapeutic and calming.

4. Building a New Identity: Developing passions outside of shopping helps redefine your self-image.

Ideas for Shopping-Free Hobbies

- Creative Outlets: Painting, writing, photography, or music.

- Fitness and Wellness: Yoga, running, hiking, or dance.

- DIY and Home Projects: Gardening, home decor, or refurbishing furniture.

- Community Activities: Volunteering, joining clubs, or participating in local events.

How to Find the Right Hobby

- Think About What Excites You: What activities have you always wanted to try?

- Experiment: Try different hobbies until you find something that resonates with you.

- Join a Group or Class: Being part of a community adds motivation and accountability.

By embracing hobbies, you replace shopping with fulfilling activities that enhance your well-being and sense of purpose.

Practicing Minimalism: Learning to Live with Less

Minimalism isn't about deprivation—it's about intentionally choosing what adds value to your life while eliminating the unnecessary. Adopting a minimalist mindset can help free you from shopping addiction and promote a more balanced and stress-free lifestyle.

The Benefits of Minimalism

1. Financial Freedom: Spending less on unnecessary items leads to savings and financial security.

2. Reduced Stress: Owning fewer possessions leads to a more organized and peaceful environment.

3. More Time and Energy: Less shopping and clutter mean more time for meaningful activities.

4. Increased Gratitude: Appreciating what you already have leads to greater contentment.

Steps to Embrace Minimalism

1. Declutter Your Space: Get rid of items you don't use or need.

2. Adopt a 'One In, One Out' Rule: If you buy something new, donate or sell an old item.

3. Prioritize Quality Over Quantity: Invest in essentials that last instead of accumulating low-quality goods.

4. Create a Capsule Wardrobe: Limit your clothing collection to versatile, timeless pieces.

5. Reduce Digital Clutter: Unsubscribe from marketing emails and social media accounts that encourage consumerism.

Minimalist Shopping Habits

• Ask Yourself If It's a True Need: Before purchasing, consider if the item is essential.

• Delay Gratification: Follow the 48-hour rule before buying non-essentials.

• Appreciate What You Already Own: Regularly take inventory of your possessions to avoid unnecessary purchases.

Minimalism shifts the focus from accumulating possessions to living a more intentional, fulfilling life.

Celebrating Small Wins and Maintaining Long-Term Progress

Overcoming shopping addiction is a journey, and celebrating progress—big or small—keeps motivation high. Recognizing your achievements builds confidence and reinforces positive financial habits.

Why Celebrating Small Wins Matters

1. Encourages Long-Term Commitment: Acknowledging progress keeps you focused on your goals.

2. Boosts Self-Esteem: Success, no matter how small, builds confidence in your ability to control spending.

3. Creates a Positive Feedback Loop: Celebrations reinforce new, healthier behaviors.

Ways to Celebrate Without Spending

• Track Your Progress: Keep a journal or use an app to note improvements in spending habits.

• Reward Yourself Creatively: Treat yourself with a relaxing bath, a nature walk, or a homemade meal.

• Share Your Success: Talk to supportive friends or join online communities focused on financial freedom.

• Reflect on Your Achievements: Regularly remind yourself how far you've come and the benefits of overcoming shopping addiction.

Maintaining Long-Term Progress

• Continue Learning: Read books, listen to podcasts, or follow financial wellness blogs.

• Revisit Your Goals: Periodically check your financial and personal growth goals.

• Stay Accountable: Partner with a friend or mentor who supports your journey.

• Be Kind to Yourself: If you slip up, don't dwell on guilt—focus on getting back on track.

By celebrating small victories and maintaining focus, you create a sustainable and rewarding path toward a balanced, shopping-free life.

Conclusion

Building a sustainable and balanced lifestyle requires shifting priorities, developing fulfilling hobbies, embracing minimalism, and celebrating progress. By focusing on experiences over material possessions, replacing shopping with meaningful activities, and reinforcing positive financial habits, you'll create a life of financial freedom, purpose, and long-term happiness.

Conclusion

Reviewing Your Journey from Point A to Point B

Overcoming shopping addiction is a transformative journey, one that requires self-awareness, discipline, and perseverance. As you reflect on your progress, it is essential to recognize how far you have come—from uncontrolled spending and emotional dependency on shopping to a place of financial stability and emotional well-being.

Key Milestones in Your Transformation

1. Recognizing the Problem: Understanding that your shopping habits were harmful and taking the self-assessment quiz to gauge the severity of your addiction.

2. Identifying Triggers: Discovering the emotional, environmental, and psychological triggers that led to overspending and impulse shopping.

3. Setting Clear Financial Goals: Developing a strong "why" for overcoming shopping addiction and creating a vision for a healthier financial future.

4. Budgeting and Tracking Expenses: Learning how to take control of your finances through budgeting strategies, delayed gratification, and responsible spending habits.

5. Changing Shopping Habits: Distinguishing between needs and wants, eliminating unnecessary purchases, and developing healthier behaviors.

6. Overcoming Emotional Dependence: Finding new coping mechanisms, practicing mindfulness, and building a strong support system to manage emotional triggers.

7. Eliminating Debt and Staying Debt-Free: Understanding the consequences of shopping-related debt, creating a repayment plan, and avoiding future financial pitfalls.

8. Building a Balanced Lifestyle: Shifting focus to experiences, adopting minimalism, and developing hobbies that provide fulfillment without financial burden.

How to Keep Moving Forward

• Revisit Your Goals Regularly: Financial and personal growth is a continuous process. Regularly reviewing your objectives will keep you on track.

• Continue Learning: Educate yourself on financial wellness through books, courses, and mentorship.

• Celebrate Small Wins: Every step forward is an achievement worth recognizing. Reward yourself in non-material ways to reinforce positive behaviors.

Your journey from point A (high addiction) to point B (freedom from compulsive shopping) is a remarkable accomplishment. The key to long-term success lies in maintaining these habits and continuously striving for financial and emotional stability.

Staying Committed to Your Financial and Emotional Well-Being

Breaking free from shopping addiction is not just about stopping excessive spending; it's about cultivating a lifestyle that supports financial health, emotional stability, and personal growth. Staying committed to these changes is crucial for long-term success.

Strategies for Long-Term Commitment

1. Create a Relapse Prevention Plan:

• Identify warning signs of slipping back into old habits.

• Develop coping strategies for handling emotional triggers without shopping.

• Have an accountability partner who can support you in staying on track.

2. Maintain a Financial Routine:

• Continue tracking your expenses and reviewing your budget.

• Set financial goals that evolve with your needs (e.g., saving for a home, investing, building an emergency fund).

• Use budgeting tools or apps to stay disciplined.

3. Practice Mindful Consumption:

• Before purchasing, ask yourself: Do I truly need this? How will this add value to my life?

• Implement the 48-hour rule before making non-essential purchases.

• Unsubscribe from marketing emails and avoid browsing shopping sites for leisure.

4. Find Fulfillment in Non-Material Aspects of Life:

• Engage in meaningful activities such as volunteering, fitness, creative hobbies, and spending quality time with loved ones.

- Focus on personal growth, relationships, and experiences rather than accumulating possessions.
- Regularly express gratitude for what you have instead of seeking happiness in material things.

Handling Setbacks

Even with the best intentions, setbacks can happen. If you find yourself slipping back into impulsive shopping habits, don't be discouraged. Instead, use it as an opportunity to reflect and reset:

- Acknowledge the slip without guilt—mistakes are part of the learning process.
- Analyze what triggered the behavior and take steps to avoid similar situations in the future.
- Recommit to your goals and revisit the strategies that have helped you succeed so far.

Long-term success requires ongoing dedication, but by staying mindful and committed, you will continue to thrive financially and emotionally.

Final Words of Encouragement

Overcoming shopping addiction is a significant achievement, and you should be incredibly proud of the effort you have put into transforming your life. Change is never easy, but you have proven that it is possible.

Remember:

- You Are in Control: You have the power to make conscious financial decisions that align with your values and goals.

- **Progress Over Perfection:** The journey to financial freedom is not about being perfect; it's about consistently making better choices.

- **Your Worth Is Not Defined by Material Possessions:** True happiness and fulfillment come from within, not from what you own.

Your journey does not end here—it is a lifelong commitment to mindful consumption, emotional well-being, and financial independence. Each day presents a new opportunity to reinforce positive habits and create a future that is free from the burdens of compulsive shopping.

As you move forward, embrace this new chapter with confidence and determination. You have taken control of your life, and the best is yet to come!

Printed in Dunstable, United Kingdom

64089360R00040